Upside Down

(a collection of poetry & thoughts)
2018-2023

M.H. John

For those who find themselves lost at sea, caught in the whirlpools of life.

May these pages be a haven, connecting our shared chaos and beauty.

Me, Myself, and Poetry | The Beginning

I began writing poetry at a pretty young age, I always say it's one of the first things I ever learned to do that really just stuck with me throughout life. I can remember being in first or second grade and reading the poem "Tell Me" from the book, "Where the Sidewalk Ends," by Shel Silverstein, and just being so captivated by the satire and harmony that the poem captured. There was just something about that poem and its meaning…wanting to be told all these beautiful things but yet also wanting to be told the truth about yourself just broke 7-year-old me down, but also made me start to realize the different elements that make up poetry. Fast forward 10 years, at 17, I really began to use writing poetry as a form to express my thoughts, emotions, mind, and overall everything. If I'm being honest, I felt like life was over for me during this time period…I think I would also hope for it to be over at times. I was going through a lot of deep personal shit around this time that just made me lose myself in the worst way possible and aside from being in therapy and having a great amount of support around me, I just couldn't find the hope in anything. I would come home from school and sleep till it was dark out and stay up and just write, cry, and read until 3-4 a.m. Moving a couple more years ahead, at 20 years old I went through yet another insane transitional period (that was very much needed). However, during this time, I had nothing but hope…I wanted to get better and be better for myself, the only thing is, I didn't know where to start. I remember one night during the summer of 2022, after recently just moving back into my parent's house, I decided to go through some boxes I had in my closet. Opening these boxes, I found journals and loose papers that I had genuinely forgotten I had written in. While reading through these pages and pages of my own thoughts, emotions, fears, and overall everything…I felt like I knew who I was for a second. Every box I had shrunk myself to fit into suddenly just fell apart and I was finally exposed to this person I was longing so hard to be…It no longer felt like I was standing in front of a stranger. Throughout reading my own personal writings, I saw the many different journeys I voyaged through, from being thrown into waters to learning to swim and eventually getting tired to letting myself drown, only to be reborn a different version again. Whether the version was for the best or not, reading through every single one of my own writings helped me gain a deep, introspective view of the kind of person I am building myself to be.

Table of Contents

Earthquake

Looking Through the Broken Mirror | Journal Entry

In 2018, when I was 16 years old, I began experiencing severe anxiety and depression. It was the strangest feeling I had ever encountered, and I wasn't sure how to deal with it. My chest would ache, and my emotions and thoughts felt as if they were floating in space, leaving me to walk around in a daze almost daily. I admit, I was terrified of what was happening to me. I started going to therapy because of this, along with other issues that we'll circle back to. However, I found that therapy only provided temporary relief, and looking back now, I realize it was because I was practically refusing to put in the work to truly confront my trauma, emotional issues, fears, and the complexities of my heart and mind. Essentially, I wasn't allowing myself to fall into the depths of my own pain, and the truth is, I couldn't stand myself.

I remember thinking, "If I can't stand myself now, why would I want to spend my time digging deeper to discover more about this person?" It felt like living inside a stranger's home… and mind.

I've always written poetry, journaled, painted—essentially, I've always taken the creative route when it comes to my personal interests and hobbies. However, it wasn't until last year (2023) that I discovered how writing poetry and journaling can be so healing for the emotions, mind, body, and soul. Because of this, I feel like I'm beginning to see and experience the beauty of life. Of course, I still deal with mental health challenges, social issues, physical struggles, and emotional hurdles—just to name a few—that I may not have the best coping skills for. But the beauty in that is that I'm figuring it out. Just like you, we're all simply here, floating along these coastal shores together, with no control over the currents of the water.

Upside Down

The stars seem to be falling at a faster pace.
I can't tell if my vision is hazy,
Or if the clouds are lifting me away
Outside of my mind, to an unfamiliar place.
I can see myself standing on the ground.
I try to call out my own name to ask for help,
But every time I open my mouth,
It doesn't let me release
A scream, a cry, or plea for help.
The skies are spinning,
The moon is falling,
I can feel my blood flowing.
However, in the midst of all this chaos,
The only thing hard for me to comprehend
Is breathing.

Seashells

Black circles traced his eyes,
And a headache that lasted for days.
He forgot all he used to be,
Lost inside foggy memories.
Replacing his lonely nights
With tears for company,
He took all he had in sight,
And soon went missing, you see
Not from the world,
But from himself.
Smoking sativa,
To try and find some help.
A backpack full of broken dreams,
And bottled memories, overflowing,
Was all he had to his name.
He crushed them all,
And fed them to the seas,
Waiting for the waves to churn,
And turn them into seashells,
Hoping in time he'd learn
To break free from his emotional spells.

Bedroom Walls

If the walls of my bedroom could talk,
They'd explain how I cry to the moon,
Holding my breath,
Giving myself chest pain,
Convincing my brain
That it's from the novocaine
I force myself to take.
Because nowadays,
I have to numb myself
To be washed in the memory
Of your acid rain.
Because it still lives inside me
The violent winds and rain, storming away,
Anytime I choose
To speak your name.

Writing Thoughts on the Bathroom Wall While Taking a Hot Shower

I step into the hot shower
For about an hour,
Giving myself 10 seconds to cry
Before falling to the floor,
Pulling the curtain liner,
Praying to the faith
Of my surrender.

I hope it happens soon;
I hope the water
Can be the one to love me,
To wrap me in its arms tightly
Enough to pull me under.

The tornado inside that's terrorized my mind
Lets the whirlwind of highs
Project violet skies
That now only live with you
In the white noise
Of heaven's sunrise.

I wanted to go out
The way you did,
But sometimes God laughs at the plans
You make out to die.

Breaking Point

I apologize to myself for falling into this again.
It took forever to recover, but only 5 seconds to break.
I'm drained.

Mourning Mirror

Each morning, I awaken only to die again
In the shadows of yesterday's dreams.
The weight of the world presses down,
Anxiety bursting at the seams.

The dawn breaks, but light doesn't follow.
My heart beats heavy inside my hollow chest.
Impending doom whispers in silence,
Turning moments of peace into unrest.

Eyes open to a familiar dread.
The sun rises, yet darkness stays—
A heavy mist clouds my mind.
Can I have a day where I wake up okay?

In the quiet of the early hours,
When the world is still asleep,
I face the mirror of my fears
And silently, I weep.

Red Sea

I can feel myself
Being swallowed by the Red Sea.
The salt water fills my eyes,
And I can no longer see.

This happens every time

I am stuck
In the whirlpool
Of my own anxiety.

I try to kick my feet,
But only tangle them more
In the seaweed that lies beneath.

Relentless

I tried to piece together the fragments
Of who I could be, or what my situation could mean.
But no matter how hard I force the puzzle pieces to click,
The jagged edges never seem to let them fit.

Every time I think I'm whole,
The cracks widen more, and more, letting in the cold.
I scream at silence, I beg every God for peace,
But my subconscious thoughts
Only seem to mock my pleas…

I try to forget, to let go,
But these memories, they just won't slow.
Every step forward feels like a lie,
Because the past pulls me back, no matter how hard I try.

Stranger's Eyes

The light in people's eyes
Who have dealt with loneliness
Glows brighter than the others
Because they have had to find conversations
Within looking up at the moon.

Gravity

Who are you
To hold so much power
Over my gravity, hour by hour?
That when I walk, I feel upside down,
Caught in your pull, I think I am about to drown.

-a letter to my anxiety

The Moon + The Tide

The moon pulled the tide
To new heights of extreme.
Scared to come down, the ocean forgot all he is
And all that he used to be.
Lost in the waves, he drifted away without a sound,
Until the sun came around
And brought the tide back down.

Washing up on another part of shore,
Under blankets of seafoam, he finds a seashell
And holds it against his ear,
Hearing his own beauty. The ocean felt profound,
And thanked the sun for bringing him
Back to the ground.

"Don't worry," said the moon,
"I'll be back tomorrow for another round."

Escape Pt. I

I was once a sailboat,
Drifting away from the only shore I knew
And the only shore
I was comfortable with.
Excited to sail on what I thought
Would be a beautiful journey
Across the seven seas.

I ended up in the middle of the ocean,
With no lighthouse, no wind to navigate my sail,
No destination.
Afraid of the isolation,
I tied my hands and feet together
And plunged to the bottom
Of the Emerald Sea,
Hoping to escape my mind's confusion.

Narcissism

Is this what my purpose in life
Was planned to be all along?
Trying to please and appease
Someone with a twisted disease,
Who holds the keys to my emotions,
Turning the lock anytime
They see me happy.

I shattered myself, hiding away,
Masking my feelings,
Becoming more numb day by day.
I molded into their desired shape
And set myself on fire
From their ego's fuel of hate.

I let myself be watched
Through the glass of a two-sided mirror
By a sociopath,
Wasting my spirit away.
I beg for acceptance, for them to stay.
But there's nothing in this world I can do
To let the narcissist know
That much like them, I am hurting too.

Echoes

Each Morning,
I awaken,
Only to die in the shadows of yesterday's dreams.

Drowning in Bubbles

I stood over the sink,
Waiting for it to fill,
To wash away yesterday's tears,
To cleanse my face of sorrow.

Suddenly, your words,
They gripped my neck tight,
Submerging me underwater, out of your sight.
Every hateful word,
Muffled beneath the surface.
When I pulled up,
The sink was filled with bubbles,
Your silent apology for today,
Until it happens again tomorrow.

Groundless

My outer body experiences
Feel more normal to me
Than planting my own two feet on the ground
And walking.

See You Soon…

Packing for a change,
I'm floating off into a different place.

Luggage tags and duffle bags, I'll be there soon.
Flying into the sky,
To live with you in the clouds.
My goodbyes are final,
My bags have been checked.

I'll see you soon,
So we can fly together into the moon.

Lullaby

My tears
Are the only ones
Who ever sing me to sleep.

Amusement *Park*

If life was like a rollercoaster,
I'd be stuck at the top,
Because I am too scared of the downward drop.
I always think to myself,
"What if there won't be another way up?"

Summer Dragonfly

Summer dragonfly,
How I stare and watch you fly by.
One of your wings is broken, yet somehow
You find the strength to fly
The skies of my mind.
However, for some reason,
You never fly to me in reality,
To help me find my inner strength
Whenever I forget about
Who I am and cry.

Especially late at night,
When I'm sitting in the meadow, surrounded by
1,000 fireflies questioning why,
Why did God have to give me this life?
I know these questions
Aren't supposed to be spoken aloud,
Mostly because if He truly can hear me,
He would be proud of how
I ask for ways,
Ways for Him to take my breath away.

Summer dragonfly,
Won't you flutter my way,
To help me mend my own broken wings?
I know that I broke them from helping others
To learn to fly before me,
But now,
I am ready to fly away from

The land of 1,000 fires,
Because the temperature gauge within my brain
Is only rising higher and higher.

I beg of you, please,
Summer dragonfly,
In a world full of hatred and rage,
Transfer your healing energy into me,
And help remove me from my skin,
As you do yourself,
To be born into the person
I know I am meant to be,
And to open my heart,
So I may love, and finally be
Genuinely happy…

What the Water Has Brought Me

The water never gave me much
Except for pain.
Each time I catch myself crying,
Whispering your name,
I draw a bath to soak away
The emotional strain.

As I slip under warm hues,
I'm welcomed by tearful arms,
Words said by none other than you.
Within the depths of my mind, I sit and sink,
Confronting thoughts as I ponder and think:
How can I be the one
To now save me?

-a poem inspired by Ms. Frida Kahlo's painting, "What the Water Gave Me"

Inverted

Can You Read My SOS? | Journal Entry

Now, I feel it's only right to open the stained glass windows of my soul and give you a little more insight into myself, my heart, and a glimpse into my experiences in love. Picking up from the last journal entry, "Looking Through the Broken Mirror," I started talking about how I began experiencing anxiety and depression at a young age. There have been a number of factors that I have endured that caused my brain to start releasing emotional pain so young, but one factor I found to be the most common…was love. In hopes of finding at least 1/4th of myself, I began reading through every single journal I own that is completely full front to back. But there was one entry in particular that stuck out to me that I feel fully represents my experience in love…

To me, it can be described as being in the middle of the emerald green sea, on a white boat, with the person that ignites you and your emotions the most. However, at some point together while out at sea…lonely…you know that same, igniting person is going to hold you until you are fast asleep and then they are going to tie your hands together and throw you overboard… now you're using the power of your own two feet for yourself and wellbeing. In the middle of the emerald green sea, your chest is open and your heart's pain mixes with the waves, washing you in the color red. Your body fills with water but it doesn't weigh you down, instead it helps you float…barely enough to keep your eyes above water level. Although you won't be able to breathe, you'll be able to see. Soon, you'll realize that although breathing another human's air can be amazing…it's all sublime and your moral sense of direction is far more divine.

In the end, you know I am too vulnerable
To be riding our ocean waves alone…
Could you read my SOS? Can you be the one
To signal me back home?

Nothing Gold Can Stay

I cried over you while sitting in the rain today

My tears mixed with the water droplets,

Expecting them to be washed away

They began to flood at my feet, causing a swimming pool of remorse to form before me.

The rain poured down, relentless, as if it knew my heart was broken,

Every tear I shed, a piece of me falling apart,

The storm inside grew stronger, mirroring my heart,

I stood there drenched, feeling exposed,

Wishing the rain could cleanse this ache,

My heart is now enclosed to the way life's pain

Comes and goes…

Nothing surprises me anymore,

I'm familiar with every ache

And every way possible that you would expect

A heart to break

And truthfully, it's been a long time

Since I've begun feeling this way

What's different now, is that I don't have you here

To hold me, and guide me, and let me know that eventually I'll be okay.

I should've listened when they told me

That in life,

Nothing gold can stay.

Hallucinating Happiness

I haven't been able to get out of bed lately,
And it's not because I don't want to
Or that I'm feeling lazy,
But because after I'm done crying
I hallucinate, and see your face in the ceiling, and for a moment, I feel happy.
Until I feel the soft warmth
Of my tear-stained pillow case,
How will I be able to find you again
When the world is colored in a single shade of gray?
I take the blood from the cracks of my broken heart
To paint your smile, which is a work of art,
So it may light my way through the blackened out thoughts
That has taken over my mind today.
As I linger in this bed,
Unable to move,
I replay the consistent thought of how I hope
Every now and then
You still think of me too…

Warnings of a Stranger

My mother always warned me
About what to do
If a stranger ever tries
To come up
And talk to you

But she never warned me of how

The body you lay with
The second soul
You choose to bear can become a stranger
At the drop of a star as well.

Orchid Oil Tears

My beloved,
You don't seem to see
How you've taken everything from me
Leaving my secrets
Spilled out in blue ink;
Like orchid oil tears
The sweet aroma of fear,
Extracted by you,
Fills my world
And I can no longer think.

Petals on My Skin

They tell me you hit me

Because you care,

But love shouldn't bruise; it shouldn't tear.

However, for me, it's much deeper

Then the love bites you leave,

Blue hydrangea marks,

Their petals fall on my skin before me.

These seasonal kisses,

From a love so untrue,

Remind me every springtime of the pain caused by you.

Fruitful Tears

I cried this morning
While washing my fruits
My tears mingling with water
Fixated on conversating
About my emotions
Simply due to the fact
That everything in my garden was grown by
The love of me

Only to be harvested
On a regular sunny Tuesday afternoon
By none other

Then the hands of you.

What To Do When Your Lover No Longer Wants You
(A guide)

1. Take shelter in your room
2. Open your blinds...only at night
3. Stare at the moon
4. Avoid mirrors!
5. Look at every Polaroid and cry...just fucking cry
6. Repeat step 5, but with love letters...add fire
7. This is where the pain sets in...take a hot shower for an hour
8. Self-soothe every morning while getting ready
9. Self-loath every night (however long you feel is right)
10. Learn how to get rid of the blank stare when hearing their name...it's noticeable
11. Ask questions, don't beg for answers (to yourself and god only. Even though you know you shouldn't)
12. Don't listen to their favorite music...you didn't like it anyway
13. Allow yourself to feel, however, it's your right
14. Continue loving... it won't hurt forever

-a poem inspired by Ms. Rupi Kaur

We Fell in Love in October

Maybe we loved each other
Most in the fall because, much like us
The flowers were dying.

Held By the Tides of You

Every time I fall in love,

The sea salt water fills my lungs a little bit more,

Until eventually, I find myself lying on the ocean's floor.

The tidal waves of love pull me down into

The silent depths of the dark blue,

Where the temperature of the water reminds me of the cold bare hands of you.

In the fog of the marine layer where your shadow resides, I lose myself in the strength of your tide.

Captured by the weight of your silent plea,

I'm drowning in a love that won't set me free…

Eclipse

I hope he can be the one
Who brings you coffee
At two in the afternoon
When you finally awake
From being up all night

Talking to the moon

About how you feel the sunshine, but can't find the light,
How there's constantly
A solar eclipse
That overshadows your mind.

Revive

I attempted to cry for you,
Because I was always taught
That if you add water
To a dead flower,
It could come back to life,
But my tears were not enough.

Golden Bloom

I woke up this morning

To a single sun ray

Shining through into my room.

As it danced on my wall, a golden bloom,

I found myself opening my eyes to having different thoughts of you.

My quiet heart began echoing

As I gazed upon your side of the bed,

Everything untouched, our sheets still tucked beneath your pillow case, where you once laid.

The emptiness spoke volumes to me,

So loud and clear,

And a reminder of how you left us lonely

In a bed full of stars, my dear.

How Summers Changed

The summers haven't been the same since you left.
Late at night
I drive to the beach
And listen to the violence of the waves
Because I remembered how,
About a year ago today,
A psychic told me that if I changed my mindset
But keep me in one place,
In the sounds of them crashing
I'd be able to hear you calling my name.

Burying myself on land
In front of the sea before me,
I grip the sand,
Feeling the grains slip through my fingers
One by one,
As if your hand is letting go,
I gather every seashell I can
To place them beneath your star
In hopes that you'll see them from afar
And notice that even though we're far apart

It's you
Who still wades in the waters of my heart.

Wilting

I tried to pull all of the sunshine
Out of the sky
And all of the water
Out of the ocean
To pour into your veins,
So that it may get the blood
Of our memories flowing back into
The roots of your heart
In hopes that it could
Bring the dead parts of our petals back to life.

Satin Blue

Every memory
I've had of you
Has unwillingly found its way
Back to me
Turning what was once

Our white silk sheets
Into satin blue

Every tear stain, a different thread
Embroidered with every

I love you
We had ever said

To each other.

On Fire

I put my heart on my sleeve.
Then you came along,
And set my sleeve on fire.

Escape Pt. II

I tried to sail away
Across the seas of make believe to escape,
or find the answer to
This fucked up reality.
But, halfway through my voyage,
The seaweed entangled me,
Anchored by memories,
I can't break free
The waves whisper your name,
Hauntingly,
Echoing the pain that still rages inside of me.

Melting

I turned the sun
And melted myself
Over the moon
Hoping to make
My heart bright enough
To shine home to you…

Colors Pt. I

One pill,
Two pill,
Three pill,
Four,

Some numb a little some numb more

Red
Purple
Orange
And blue,

These are the colors
That keep me company
To distract myself from the thoughts of You.

Mars

I think you and I
Would grow much better
Together on Mars.

We have already taken up
Too much of each other's
Oxygen, anyway.

Explaining Heartbreak to a Five Year-Old

(A concept poem)

I drove to the park after it rained,

Got out of my car, sat on the bench, and stared at my reflection while crying today.

With my AirPods in my ears and my hands gripping my hair, I feel a tap on my leg.

Glancing to the side, a ball sits at my feet,

I can see a little boy out of the corner of my eye running up to me.

"Mister! Mister! Could you roll my ball back over here, please?"

But, the cracking of my heart, voices of my thoughts, and screams of my tears Were too loud for me to hear.

Placing my hands over my eyes to create a sense of darkness So that I may think clearly…I feel a tap on my shoulder.

Wiping my tears before I turn around,

I'm greeted by the little boy;

"Hi, mister…I'm sorry if my ball hitting you made you cry".

"No, buddy," I responded.

"Your ball hitting me didn't make me cry…in fact, it kind of made me laugh, which I needed…thank you for that", I continued saying.

"But, mister, why are you crying? I know today wasn't a perfect day…but the sun is out now,

You should enjoy it and play", he says to me.

Before I explain my heartbreak,

I take a minute to pray that he will never have to experience pain like this at such a young age…unlike myself.

"You're right, buddy. Today wasn't a perfect day…but now it is…

Remember how, for most of the day, the clouds covered the sun
and created a different type of shade that was just a little
too…dark?
The sun in my heart has also gone away,
And the rainbows aren't reaching far enough to wash me in color,
And without color, how can I have fun?"
"I understand, mister," the little boy says, running off
But still kicking the ball my way.

Disposable Camera

You brought me along
For the journey,
And after I developed
And gave you memories
You discarded me.

Mosaic

Mirrored fragments catch the light,
Moments captured,
Day and night.
In every shard,
Your soul, I see,
For truthfully, *it is you*
Who completes
The mosaic of me.

Ferris Wheel

We sat in empty parking lots
And watched the ferris wheel go around,
Talking about how
We were once
On top of the world together,
And now, at the bottom,
Exiting the ride,
But still syncing our heartbeats to the neon lights.

Swan Song

We wrote our songs
In the stars
For the gods to sing,
But we wrote it out of tune,
And maybe that's why
The universe
Couldn't save us.

Storm in the Frame

You came to our blank canvas
With black and blue paints in hand,
Trying to create a sunset out of my soul,
But all you painted was a whirlpool
A chaotic cycle, consuming us whole.
Each brush stroke
A turbulence of disarray,
Which only further causes me
To lose my way…
But still, you framed it and hung it on a wall
Trapping me in the center, making me feel small.

Homesick

Why do I feel lost, away from a home
That never truly felt like mine
A home that was crowded with people
Yet, I always felt so alone inside?

I guess that it's my fault
For laying the foundation as my heart
Because each time you set it on fire
It melts me into the concrete…

A new floor for you to walk all over,
You and your perfect family.

Five Stages of Grief When Losing Someone Alive

Denial:

I tell myself

They just needed a break

A vacation for the day but then a day turns into a week, and a week into a lifelong stay.

I keep believing they'll be back,

That this is just a phase,

Ignoring missed calls and empty texts, lost in a hopeful haze.

All my questions remained unanswered,

Wrapped in cellophane,

Hoping they'll return

To ease my silent pain.

Anger:

I rage at the world,

For them running away, every little thing annoys me, in the most unexpected way.

I curse at the silence

That fills in their empty space, and the memories that haunt me, in every familiar place.

I blame them for leaving,

But myself for the pain,

Caught in a storm of fury, that falls like endless rain.

Bargaining:

This is where the *"what ifs"* come into play,
And how the *"what ifs"* create a fake display.
A world of imagination,
A fake escape from the pain.
I replay every moment,
Wondering what I could trade,
To turn back the time,
For the choices that were made.
I whisper to the stars,
And plead with the night,
Offering my soul,
To make everything right.

Depression:

These blackout curtains
Still aren't dark enough for me, your face in the shadows,
is all I seem to see.
In every picture frame,
Your smile's still hanging there,
A haunting presence, lingering in the air.
Your laughter echoes softly,
In the silence of my room,
A constant reminder of how now
I'm only one of two.

Acceptance:

Now I finally feel alive,
And somewhat free, the sun is no longer my enemy
But now a friend, though bittersweet,
Reminding me each day,
That I am alive,
But in a quiet, lonely way.
Content, yet haunted by this,
I accept my reality
With a lingering melancholy.

After Love

There's still life
After letting go,
You just have
To be willing to
Walk the miles
Down your long, dark road.

A Letter to You…

Dear *****,

I remember the first time I ever really felt in love, it was with you. It felt like the beginning of summer, maybe because it was, but the sun's rays melted my body away, leaving my heart to be the grains of sand that constantly kept slipping through your hands. After what happened, I found myself lost, staring at the moon, thinking of the conversations we'd always have about how, even though we kept far away, we had the same lunar light to lay under at the exact same time every night so that we felt connected to each other in a different type of way. I can still recall every wish you told me, every dream you had, every nightmare that'd keep you awake on the phone with me, both of us reading each other poetry at two, three or four in the morning until we fell asleep…only I never slept because hearing you breathe over the phone was the only rest I ever needed. It's been years since you've loved me, but for me, it's only been about six months since I last told myself that I love you. It wasn't something easy for me to do; in fact, you wouldn't believe how hard I try to distract myself from any thought of you; I can't look at the stars or go on late night drives down the highway anymore because every time I do it seems as if the airwaves align, because they only play your favorite songs and all I can do is wipe the tears from my eyes. I've moved around so many times, from so many head spaces to emotions to environments, but none of them gave me the perspective of self reflecting the way you did the night you told me you couldn't take me back. It opened my eyes, but closed my heart, to the theory I had of you and not being able to fight the secret demons you keep in the dark. I hope you find peace, because I now have, now that I've learned that it can only come from within me.

Love always, Me.

Level Flight

Naval Boarding | Journal Entry

Over the last two years or so, I have done a lot of self discovery, reflecting, and growing. I can't explain how many times I thought I found myself just to further uncover that I still had (and have) thousands of layers to unwrap and mine through. There have been countless times when I felt "content" with the person I was, only to kill him off and restart the process with the idea in mind of "let's not do that again." However, during these times, I found that the same shark infesting my waters, besides myself, was my trauma. I like to think I'm a pretty self-aware person. I can feel every little minor change from the outside world to my personal inside world. What I found to be the most interesting discovery was the fact that I knew I had these traumatizing situations, experiences, and people to personally face and deal with in my private time (therapy, journaling, etc.…), but instead, I was letting this trauma control my life rather than letting myself control the trauma. The thing with trauma is it's very calculated… sure when it's an event such as a car crash or war, trauma can be a little easier to comprehend and deal with… but when trauma has a heart and brain and tears…that's where it's tricky to navigate through. What I've learned in dealing with trauma like this is that you have to 99% let yourself die when you're allowing this to happen, when you're letting these factors of trauma take control. I, myself, have been trauma bonded to an individual numerous times and literally thought, "How am I ever gonna live without this person? I can't even sleep at night without them next to me or texting me". However when it comes to that 1%, I have personally found it to be the very fine thin line between your heart and your brain, also known as the decision on if you're living your lifestyle for you or for your handler. Trauma, to me, is a pothole on your highway. I like to think of it as a pothole on a highway because you're forced to face it head on, and once you hit it hard enough, you're gonna want to redirect your course because the thought of hitting another pothole a mile down the highway is too anxiety inducing.

Gardening

The clouds above my head
Let the raindrops fall
Onto the scars of my trauma
So that they may
Grow flowers big enough
To hide the pain.

LA and How I Love You

I'm writing to you from the heart of L.A.

Because my healing process just isn't going the way I imagined.

I'm having trouble, you see,

With shedding this body, of me,

Because I can still see the imprints of your kisses and feel the soft dance of your fingertips across my skin.

I try to do anything random

To make me happy;

Driving through neighborhoods in Rosemead,

Having my chakras aligned at a random sound bath therapy,

Driving to Long Beach just to write by the sea,

Or picking lemons and oranges from the citrus trees

Within my favorite park,

Because when I pour their juices over my broken heart,

The sting brings a feeling, or a memory,

That only you could ignite in me after dark.

Everything I do, I do with the thought of you

And that's strange for me to admit because

Even after all the California earthquakes

You shifted my grounds to,

And all the pink noise I try to drown thoughts of you out to;

Like driving late at night down Sunset and Vine

While my brother talks to me

About his favorite rapper's documentary

But I'm only half listening

Because I'm too distracted

By what I've just learned about Van Gogh.

He only ever sold one painting in his lifetime

So you can imagine how emotional I get each time

I question why, why I do this

Why I try,

When nobody reads these melancholic thoughts of mine.

However, throughout all of this,

There's one thought that simply won't run away from me, it only talks about how much I love you.

Mirror

It's hard these days,
Even after all these years.
It's hard
For me to sit directly
In front of a mirror,
When all I see
In the reflection
Of the glass' tears
Is the image of you,
Replacing the body of me.

Bird World

Can you see me
From your bird's-eye view?
I stay up past three in the morning
Counting the rings of Saturn,
Crying to the moon.

I try to pray to you,

But I get lost searching
In the veins of the sky
Where the colors blend and fade
From orange to gold to purple to blue,
For the perfect star

That could possibly hold you.

Lucid Dreaming

I feel more alive
In the scenes of my dreams
Than I do in reality.
I feel your gold leaf touch
Ripple through my veins
While I call out your name
Until you come to me,
And I can see your face
Clear as day.
Before I'm able to pull you close
I feel myself float out of
The colored scenes of my dreams
And back into
The black and white
Of my reality.

Morse Code

You were a sailboat
Drifting away from a shore you once knew
And were comfortable with
Navigating the deep ocean blue,
your sail wings grew
But guided by the stars, your spirit flew.
Can you hear my adventurous heart
Signaling out to you?
My frequency is going weak,
not even in Morse code.
Can I speak across these chaotic seas?
I hope to talk to you soon,

(*I love you*)

Tearful Ashtray

If I could visit my younger self
I would go back to the day
When the laughs of lions
Didn't scare me away
Into a world

I was trying to leave astray.

A world that once

Swallowed me up whole
Making swimming pools
Out of my tears
That'd be dusted
Off of my cheek
Into the ashtrays of fools

Where the narcissists
Gather around me
To find peace,
Drinking from the sea
Of pain, they tore me apart in,
Because they only knew
What they had bled into me.

Conversations With the Moon

I think I'll stay in tonight,
And open my window to talk to the moon
Because I know she has a lot to say…
"I light up everyone's roughest nights," she tells me.
Continuing to say,
"I'm always here when they need to talk, but where are they when I need to?
When the sun rises,
They no longer talk about my beauty. I can't run from the pain it causes me, like you can.
So, I become invisible and fall to the ground
Waiting until it is my turn
To enlighten people's darkest times,
And cycle back around.
Although there are so many stars
That surround me, guiding me through
The dark side of my ecliptic heart,
I still feel so alone
Floating through my cosmic room.

Untitled

I write your name in the sand
And trace it with seashells,
Waiting for the ocean
To wash them away
Into the sea of dreams,
In hopes that it could
Bring you back to me.

Tarot Reader

In my heart of chaos, where your shadow looms,
I ventured forth, running my fastest to escape
This inevitable doom,
Also known as the thoughts of you.
No matter how fast I ran,
A storm raged on, tearing me apart,
In search of peace for my shattered heart.
I wandered through the labyrinth
Of both curiosity and despair
Seeking answers frantically, but only finding
An empty chair.
I stumble upon a dimly lit room, with cards spread wide;
A tarot reader stands before me, offering to be a guide.
As she shuffles the deck, with hands so wise,
Gazing deeply into my watery eyes, she said
"Your past is a ghost unlaid, its whispers haunt the choices you've
made."
I sit in silence, looking to the ground,
My lips become query, my hands start to shake
Not because of fear, or the truth that was just announced,
But because she has figured out the facade
I have put into place…

Life Raft

You tied my hands together

And sailed me out to sea

Throwing me into the ocean, you told me I had to learn to save myself

Before I could save you.

The waves crashed over me like a symphony of despair,

I fought against the currents, gasping for air…

But even as I struggled, only your voice echoed in my mind,

A silent plea for help, impossible to leave behind.

I reached out through the darkness

My strength, nearly gone,

Hoping to pull you from the depths,

To where we both belong.

Colors Pt. II

You took pills
To take your thoughts away.
Red, violet, and blue
Were your favorite colors,
You say.
But little do you know that the
Red, violet, and blue
Powdered, pressed hues
Are what took
Your life away.

Shipwreck

You've sailed the deepest seas,
And have seen the most exotic islands,
However,
The most violent waves
Have left you shipwrecked.

Roses Bloom For You

I walked through my garden yesterday
And beheaded the tops of daisies
After they repeatedly called out your name.
Passing by the violets,
I take a minute to shed a few tears,
Even though they only stare at me, dazed,
I can't help but feel their immense amount of pain.
Because their purple color hues remind me
Of the scars that were left
From going through physical wars with you.
Wandering through a field of tulips,
Their petals begin to fall, exposing my truth,
Of how I still plant thoughts of you in my mind
Every spring
Because with the mix of my blue hydrangea tears,
And my blue dream,
It is the only soil rich enough to keep the lilacs in my mind
Blooming beautifully from time to time.
As I stand quietly, feeling the north breeze,
Two white butterflies flutter to me
To lead me down a path in this floral maze,
Taking me to an area overcrowded by weeds and shadowed by
trees
A single rose appears before me.
Picking it, I am pricked by the thorns built to protect
Its beautiful skin.

As I bleed, I am flooded with memories of us,
And reminded of how in this fucked up reality
Roses only bloom for you.

Dandelions

I was a dandelion
In the field of Daisies,
Waiting for you
To come along
And make a wish
Out of me.

Fly Me to the Moon

I stayed until midnight,
Standing at the bus stop, waiting
To go to the airport
To board the plane to the moon

Because I heard
That it doesn't shine as bright
Now that it has you.

Silent Sorrow of the Sun

This morning, I woke up
And realized the sun was crying,
His golden tears falling like lemon drops
From way up high.

But for some reason,

All anyone could talk about
Was how beautiful
It colored the sky.

Same Color, Different Tone

I use
All of the pain I know
Each time the seasons change

To repaint my soul

Because I know
How much you hate
The same color
In various shades of tone.

Whitewater Bay

Take a walk with me
Along whitewater bay,
I'll show you the waves of my rage
That has caused my heart
To freeze over
In such a violent way.

Make sure to bring your ice skates,
That way, when I fall again,
You'll be able to catch me,
And hold me,
This time till infinity.

We'll carve scars
Disguised as skate marks
Across the frozen layers of my heart
That creates a sideways
Number eight (∞).

Moon Flower

Last night, while sleeping
Beneath the cosmic's silver rays,
A moonflower began blooming,
Slowly unfurling,
The daze my mind is in these days.
As cosmic whispers fill the air,
I wander through a world of dreams
Where time stands still and all worries cease.
I ask myself
"Why can't life always be this pretty?"
Walking through my moonlit garden,
Of the rage that waters my inner peace,
I am quickly reminded
Of how someone like me
Can only enjoy the beauty of life
And acceptance of reality in my sleep.

Six Months Away

Six months have passed
Since you slipped away,
Yet, in my heart, the anchors of its strings
Hold you here to stay.
Though our paths diverged before you were gone,
Your voice lingers in my mind
Like a soft swan song.
In my quiet moments,
When I'm sitting on the floor at the foot of my bed,
Talking to God, asking why
He couldn't
Take me instead,
I feel your touch,
A whisper of comfort, though I never expected this to hurt so
much.
The stars seem dimmer, the nights are too long,
But your memory lights the way,
A constellation for when I'm feeling lost.

Peace Within

Day by day
I lie awake,
Sometimes I pray
For a day when you and I
Could reconcile
And everything could be okay,
And we wouldn't be stuck
In this black hole
With no moons and no stars.
I know God can hear me,
Yelling and screaming,
Asking for peace.
But how could he
Increase my peace
When peace is something that
No longer lives within me?

A Letter From Beyond

I'm sorry this world
Did not welcome you
With open arms.

Send me a letter,
When you get back home,
So I know that you're safe.

Postcard

I sent a postcard today,
But it must've lost its way,
Caught in the clouds,
Never reaching the golden gate,
Where you patiently await.
I wrote of our memories and dreams,
Hoping they'd bind the seams,
Of time and space between us,
But my words drift into the sky,
Left unsaid, unanswered, why?

Wishful Thinking

I was scrolling through my camera roll
The other day,
And found a blurry picture of you,
Because I was too lost trying to capture
The moon in frame.
I was so focused on the stars above,
Never being this far from city lights,
Distracted,
I missed the cosmic glow
That sparkled in your eyes.
Looking back, as my feet pull ahead of me,
A sea of what I failed to see
Washes over me,
The beauty of you
Reaches over and drowns me…
Our memories tumble like sea glass
In my mind,
Each piece created from the tears
We both cried,
Now, whenever I go on my late night drives,
I pull over under every shooting star
To wish you were here with me,
Right by my side.

Edens Trees

You salt my gardens green
Reviving the trees
In which Eden
Used to swing.

Calling out to me
To bring my own tears
From the emerald sea,
I give them to you to control.

For my gardens know
How I have
Lost my soul
Far too long ago.

Chameleon

Oh chameleon soul
Why must you try to
Blend into a world that won't change?
Lost in the masquerade
Shifting shapes with every grieving stage
Mirroring the world's array.
Yet in the mirror, a stranger's gaze.

You're longing for a steady hue,
A constant self,
Of wanting to be both firm and true.
Yet when fear's whispers draw the veil,
Once again, your colors return back to pale,
Revealing your true self
To those around you, no longer portraying
The act of living within a fairytale.

Not a Lover, Nor an Artist

I wrote about you for the last time today

Because I can no longer take the way

My heart breaks each time I turn my tear-stained pages…

The ink smudges and fades, leaving behind only empty spaces

In places, I always thought your name would remain permanently engraved.

The stars fall rapidly out of the sky

To symbolize the way

These pent-up emotions I have of you,

Boil over on my insides, causing tears to rush out of my eyes.

I've kept you alive in every line,

Yet lately, when I write,

I find myself crossing out stanzas where I have you in mind.

I remember reading a quote one day that said something like

When an artist loves you, they keep you alive

In every art they make, every word they rhyme,

However, when I pick up the brush to paint,

I find that the colors of you + me

Blur and fade… Maybe my love for you truly has begun to decay.

Upright

Pit Stop | Journal Entry

Sometimes, in life, when the sun starts to set just under the horizon of the sea and the sky fades from a pastel ombre to the nightly shade of black, and the moon pulls the tide closer and closer to the shore, turning it into the bay… I like to remind myself that even at night, when the beauty of the white sand beaches gets lost under the water, by day, they're whole again… with new seashells to be discovered, and the violent waves are a little bit more controlled.

One thing that I've been extremely grateful for, probably more than ever, is the present… I am the type of person who moves between two spaces in life; the past and the future. If I'm not trying to figure out, or worrying about, how I'm going to establish myself for my future, how I'm going to set myself up for comfortability, then I'm too busy drowning in my own head… to busy living in past circumstances, past emotions or trauma, or even past conversations… I guess really just self-pitting. But, recently, I've learned to make a pit stop in the present while traveling between the county lines of the past and future… and truthfully, I've been enjoying it here very much. I've been noticing such small details of life that I've looked through so many times… some even as simple as feeling which way the wind is blowing in from.

I went through a time not too long ago where I was isolating myself very much from the people around me… any time I was around anyone, it started to feel like I was suffocating and I really couldn't figure out why. Until one day, I had a conversation with someone very close to me about this topic and they pointed out that the reason for this, was that I didn't have the patience to connect with myself, and if I can't connect with myself, how am I going to find the patience to connect with these people in my life who care so much for me? Totally called me out on my bullshit…but I needed to hear it. After this conversation, I went home and sat with what was said to me and began journaling everything that was making me angry, making me frustrated, and everything that was making me feel like a hostage to my emotions… unironically, every thought and emotion that came out of me was all tied to my past somehow. So, in that moment, I made a conscious decision to purge everything that is no longer aligning with me, presently, instead of trying to align myself to my past or future…

Altogether, I am still figuring out life's beauty every single day…every time I think I've found something eye-opening, it slips away only to be replaced by something more breathtaking. I'm learning that the messiness of life, the hardships, the trials and tribulations, are also what makes life beautiful…because in every change, there's an opportunity to become more aware of every small detail of life and yourself.

The AI of Me

I got home tonight;
Walking in front of the mirror,
I undress out of my skin.

Leaving my corpse lying on the floor,
I sit next to it.

Opening my eyes
To release the water that has short-circuit
The wires of my mind,
I take a deep breath and count to three
As I gaze into the mirror depths.

Reflections of my soul emerge;
Skinless and vulnerable, I confront myself
Causing my memory to surge.

I don't recognize this person anymore.
Dropping the hard drives into the degausser;
Old files displaying,
An error occurs:
"Are you sure you want to erase memory?"

CTRL+ALT+DELETE

I have finally set myself free
Of the AI that controls my mind

Named:
Victim mentality

Sunrise

I watched the sunrise this morning
And realized that I no longer need you
To help me see the beauty within this life.
Getting ready for nothing much to do,
I brew my coffee, still, a pot for me and you,
while staring out the window, wondering what lesson
I could learn from today.
Should I take the time now to pray?
Or should I just let myself fall
Within the silver linings of the sun rays
That are shining directly onto the pool floor
And take the time to soak and meditate…
Sending my energy to whichever one of my friends
Needs it the most that day.
I could lie in the grass and count the clouds,
Not realizing how much time has truly passed.
Or I could drive to L.A. for the day
And talk on the phone with my brother
While I'm stuck in traffic on the 405 freeway,
Which truthfully, when I am in it, I never complain
Because the philosophy of life moving so fast
And suddenly being stopped by strangers in the same space
Is beautiful to me.
These are just a couple of things that I have found to be the most
beautifully intricate
Since you've forced me
To purge any old skin
That holds your memory.

Tasseography

I like my green tea with two leaves,

For when I breathe in the steam,

The camellia cleanses me

And forces my eyes to see every shadow that I've hidden deep,

Awakening truths that once did sleep.

In my cup's reflection, I see every scar,

Mapping out my journey like distant stars.

After I'm done, the remaining tea leaves tell a story

Of the person I used to be,

But they don't know,

That I've set myself free in the healing waters

That used to drown me, or that in the ocean's flow, I've found my key to unlock the door to my inner world, where my soul has longed to be unfurled.

Two leaves in my tea, a balance to find,

One for the heart

And one for the mind.

Learning to Breathe

Slow down,
Take your time and realize,
There's more to find.
Sit outside in the grass,
Feel the sun on your skin
Slowly pass.
Sometimes, you may feel like
You could fly,
Soaring high with the birds
In the sky.
But all you need to do is breathe
And you'll be grounded
With the lilacs beneath.

Seed of Peace

Last night I had a dream
That I was finally free.
Free from the burdens,
The anxiety,
The heartbreaks that changed the person
I now try to burn endlessly in the flames.
For a moment,
I felt like me,
Whoever that may be.
I felt like someone who is still
Very much a stranger to me,
And the decisions I've made.
Maybe this version of conscious
I was experiencing
Just hadn't gone through life fully,
So he was only showing me moments
Of when I'd forgotten I was happy.
Either way, I felt a little bit of peace
Inside of this R.E.M. sleep,
A feeling I hadn't felt
Since I was seventeen,
Specifically,
When I was falling deeper
And deeper in love with you
Under swaying blue cypress trees,
I felt so complete…

So, when you left,
And I awoken from my dream,
I couldn't help but ask
Everyone around me, *why?*
Why would you let this happen to me?
They explained
That in order to feel happy,
You must first feel the pain,
And within your pain,
Hides the seed of peace.
Once you plant that seed,
And nurture it,
Watering it,
Giving light to its body,
You begin to bloom into the version of yourself
You always dreamt to be…

Get Free

After climbing onto the rocks
And to the top of the cliff,
He feared now not,
Feeling the comfort
Of the whirlpool's drift.
For while standing above the sea,
He found new meaning in life,
Now that he's realized
He is free.

Everything's Okay

If you're feeling down
Or feeling blue,
Sit outside in the summer's breeze,
And listen to what
The birds sing to you.
Close your eyes
And open your mind,
Like petals in spring,
Thanking the sun,
For helping them bloom into
Their colorful beauty.

Grand Rising

This morning, I opened my eyes and stretched my limbs to the ends of my bed,

I thanked the sun

For my grand rising with him,

Brewed my coffee and began meditating under the full moon

Within my head.

It's crazy to me that this is my morning these days,

Because five years ago, exactly to the date today,

I swore that I'd be dead,

But I've found that if you let the light shine in and let every part of your being shed,

You'll be okay

You'll be okay

You'll be okay…

Acting

I used to envision myself gracing scenes
Of your spotless minds
Silver screen,
In films wrapped in gold cellophane,
Directed in flickers of light,
Electrified by pain,
Enhanced by the vision of what
Our love could be.

Switching to black & white projections
Anytime I feel happy
To play onto the theme of
My own personal defeats,
Because even the actors in this film know
I'm the happiest
When you're without me.

I Forgive You

I forgive you for the pain you caused,
For the times when love seemed lost.
I forgive you for the nights I cried,
For the moments when you lied.
I forgive you for the broken trust,
For the dreams that turned to dust.
I forgive you for the silent days,
For the hurtful words and ways.
I forgive you not for you, but me,
To set my heart and spirit free.
With forgiveness,
I find peace,
And let my soul's quiet strength increase.

Spring

Planted as a seed,
I was thrown in the dirt,
And covered,
Taking root in what was being
Poured into me,
Adapting to weather,
Eventually, learning to withstand
The hurricanes of my creator's nature.

You came to me
During spring,
Harvesting my pollen,
The air that I breathe out of me,
To help me open up and grow,
And bloom into the person I was meant to be.

(I thank you)

Developing

Sometimes, we have to soak
In the negatives
Of our celluloid scenes
In order to develop
And see the color
Within the world.

My Love...

I make love,
In my poetry and in my free time...
If you'll have it, here's my heart,
Open it to read, it's yours to keep
Or to make it bleed
Just all I ask, is please,
Love me in the way
That I know I'm meant to be.

Prism

In the garden of my heart, you bloom,
A single rose that brightens every room,
Petals soft, in colors bright,
Your love, a sunrise that blinds my eyes.
Among the tulips, red & gold,
And violets, that sing out story untold,
Your love finds me, like a prism in the rain,
Bringing the color back to my life,
Once again.

Moonlight

Maybe you couldn't sleep
Because the moons
Were trying to
Talk to you.

Shades of You

I am not an artist,
And I don't know
How to paint.

But if I were to take
All the shades of blue

And blend them together,
They would most certainly
Create a painting of you.

Watercolor

If a painting
Had your voice
I'd sit and watch it dry
For millions of years.

What Makes Me Happy...

Between you and the poetry
I'm beginning to see
Just how beautiful
Life can truly be.

Tangerine Dream

I can see
The joyful beam
Of your smile
In my tangerine dreams,
Your eyes are the sunset,
Tangled in webs of green.
The floral haze
That dances on the clouds
Come from your
Pink flower cheeks.
I never want you to leave,
I'm happy
In a way, I've never been,
For you, I do anything
Inside and outside
Of this tangerine dream.

The Moon's Beauty

What would the moon say to earth
If she discovered that your beauty
Stood flying high
While hers fell to the ground?
Would she hide
In the sun's shadow for the rest of her life?
Or would she distance herself
So far that she turns into
One of the stars
That she used to wish upon?

Eternal Sunshine

You drift through my thoughts, soft and serene,
Making the stars twinkle above,
I haven't seen them dance like this
Since I was seventeen.
In me, the tides follow the way the moon aligns
No bounds, just waves,
I'm most restless without you, at night.
Oceans grace,
Star chaser,
Holder of the equator line,
But who am I?
Just a soul in love, dreaming anew,
Rearranging the planets above for a different view…
I'm in love with you,
My silent muse,
Summers hue,
Eternal sunshine
Is what I feel when I'm melting
In the hands of you.

Time

I measure time
By the number of beats
My heart skips
The longer that I am away
From you.

Ego Death

I stood in the gentle rain
With one of my friends today.
Looking for solace,
We sit on the grass,
Holding each other,
Our tears interlace.
Lotus flowers appear
In the palm of our hands
To cleanse our souls anew,
Washing ego's away,
Embracing our truth.

Energy

Two people
Pulled together as one
From energies that combine
Controlling the currents tides,
The moon,
And the sun.

A Letter to the Universe

Dear universe,
Please let me be grounded
So your energy
May radiate through this world
And into the roots of me
That have longed
To be brought back to life.

Thankful

I'm thankful for you
And for the trees
And for the way the sun
Magnifies the ocean's beauty.
I couldn't imagine
What life would be like
If I didn't have you
Here with me.

The Blue Hummingbird

The wind blows in every direction,

But somehow, it has brought

The blue hummingbird to me.

I can see the hummingbird sitting on my bay window,

Fluttering its wings as it watches me.

I look at the hummingbird as it begins to question me.

"What do you do it for? What are you hiding from? Who are you running from?" The hummingbird asks.

"Myself,"

I say to the hummingbird

As it stares at me, continuing to flutter its wings fast enough to make my wind chime ding.

"Follow me," the hummingbird demands.

Taking me to a place where my trauma came to be.

"This is where your happiness begins," the hummingbird says to me.

"What do you mean?" I ask the hummingbird.

"This place is full of anger and rage and reminds me of people's selfish ways that instilled my hate," I say to the hummingbird.

Following, as it leads me down the hallway of memories that

Flooded by my tears from trying to escape

By sailing away.

The hummingbird looks to me and says

"This place is hell for you, isn't it?

Full of pitch-black days where you'd lie

Helplessly awake and listening to the rain,

Praying for ways, ways God could take you away?

Hell is not a place nor a certain evil,

But hell, however, lives within other people and it can come out

In ways of being deceitful.

Instead of flying as a child,

You would drown.

Not from the lack of love,

But so you couldn't feel

The pain around you."

Responding to the hummingbird, I say,

"Yes, I understand that."

Before uttering another sentence, the hummingbird flutters its wings at a faster speed

To silence me, showing a wider reality.

The hummingbird then proceeds to say to me,

"I am trying to explain that you may understand, but you cannot grasp

What is coming to be by clinging to your old energy.

You must let things go and let them be.

For I am no longer you,

And you are no longer me.

You cannot keep walking this earth

With the burden of me on your back,

Only for the fact that when you cannot sleep at night

You bring a memory of me back.

So let me go, and let yourself see

What truly matters,

For I am peaceful now

Just as you need to be."

Made in United States
Troutdale, OR
03/27/2025

30114184R00076